Furry
Creatures

Clint Twist

Author: Clint Twist
Managing Editor: Ruth Hooper
Editor: Emily Hawkins
Art Director: Ali Scrivens
Designer: Bill Mason
Picture Editor: Frances Vargo

Created and produced by
Andromeda Children's Books
An imprint of Pinwheel Ltd
Winchester House
259-269 Old Marylebone Road
London
NW1 5XJ. UK
www.pinwheel.co.uk

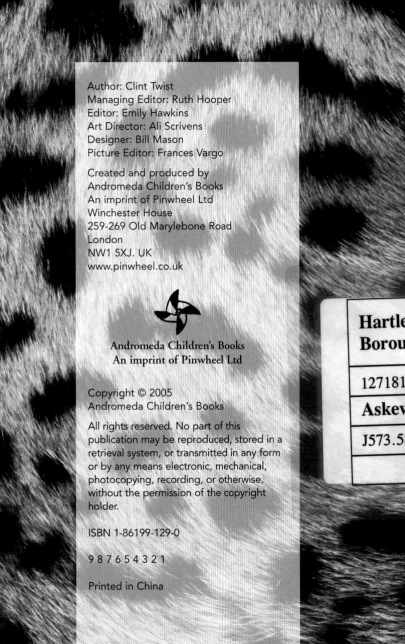

Andromeda Children's Books
An imprint of Pinwheel Ltd

ISBN 1-86199-129-0

9 8 7 6 5 4 3 2 1

Printed in China

Contents

Introduction

Many animals have coats of fur. Hairs of different lengths grow out of their skin, completely covering their bodies. Fur helps these animals in different ways – it provides warmth, camouflage and protection.

European Red Squirrel

Every tiger has a unique pattern of stripes on its face.

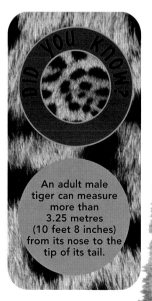

DID YOU KNOW?

An adult male tiger can measure more than 3.25 metres (10 feet 8 inches) from its nose to the tip of its tail.

A Fine Balance

The European red squirrel has a long tail covered with bushy fur. This tail helps the squirrel keep its balance while climbing along tree branches. It is also used to send messages to other squirrels.

The fur on a tiger's face is short, so it does not block its vision.

Musk Ox

A tiger has long, stiff hairs, called *whiskers*, around its nose. They are very sensitive.

Hairy Beast

The musk ox lives in the mountains of Greenland, Canada and Alaska. It has long, thick fur to protect it from snow and freezing winds. The musk ox is unusual – its fur is so long that it nearly drags along the ground.

Fierce and Furry

The tiger is the largest and fiercest of the big cats. Like other cats, it is completely covered by fur. The only bit of bare skin to be seen is on the very tip of its nose.

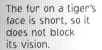

Siberian Tiger

FASCINATING FURRY FACTS

The musk ox's name suggests that it is a type of cow, but it is actually more closely related to mountain sheep.

When threatened by wolves, a group of adult musk oxen will stand in a circle around their young to protect them.

Who Is Furry?

Most mammals are furry. There are many different kinds of mammal, including bats, cats, cattle, monkeys, seals, elephants and sheep. Mammals are warm-blooded and feed milk to their young.

All-Over Fur

Like many mammals, this grey woolly monkey is almost completely covered by a thick fur coat. The only parts of its body without fur are its face, the palms of its hands and the soles of its feet.

Long fur on the monkey's body forms woolly tangles.

Fruit Bat

Partly Furry

Some mammals, such as this fruit bat, have fur on only some parts of their bodies. The wings of bats, which are actually enlarged hands, have little or no fur on them.

DID YOU KNOW?

There are over 4,450 different species of mammal, and about a quarter of these are bats.

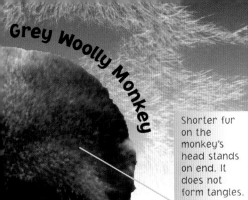

Grey Woolly Monkey

Shorter fur on the monkey's head stands on end. It does not form tangles.

FASCINATING FURRY FACT

Bats must find their way in the dark. To do this, they send out high-pitched squeaks. When the squeak hits an object, an echo bounces back. The bat can locate the object from the sound of the echo. This is called *echolocation*.

Furry or Not?

An African elephant does not look like a furry creature. It appears to be covered by wrinkled, hairless skin – there is certainly no sign of a fur coat. But actually, elephants have thick hairs growing from their skin.

An elephant's ear can be up to 1.5 metres (5 feet) long!

African Elephant

What Is Fur?

Fur is the name of the coat of hair covering the bodies of most mammals. Some mammals have only a few hairs on their bodies. Others have a type of thick fur called *wool*. The hair on a person's head is also a kind of fur.

Elephant Trunk

Elephant Fur

Some parts of an elephant's body, like the trunk, have widely spaced hairs growing from them. These hairs can be seen only from up close. They are most noticeable on young elephants – adults appear to be almost completely hairless.

FASCINATING FURRY FACTS

A newborn elephant weighs about 100 kg (220 lbs). It can start to walk within one hour of its birth.

The pine marten's diet is very varied. It eats small birds, small mammals, beetles, caterpillars, eggs and berries.

Each of the pine marten's coat hairs ends in a fine point. This makes it difficult for snowflakes to stick to its fur.

Shearing a sheep's fleece without hurting the animal is a highly skilled job. The best sheep-shearers can remove a fleece in less than a minute.

Pine Marten

Thick fur allows the pine marten to bend its legs without exposing the skin beneath.

Thick Fur

Thick fur covers the pine marten's entire body, including the soles of its feet and most of its face. This fur keeps its body warm during cold winters. The fur along the pine marten's sides and back is coloured, so it blends in among the tree branches.

Black-Faced Sheep

Wool

Sheep and goats have coats of wool. These coats are made of hairs that tangle together into a fleece. The hairs can be removed from the animal by combing or clipping. Then, they are spun together into longer, thicker fibres that can be knitted or woven to make cloth.

Why Is Fur Important?

The main purpose of fur is to keep animals warm. Mammals use some of the food they eat to produce body heat. A coat of fur helps stop this precious heat from escaping.

Polar bear fur is not pure white. It has a slight yellow tinge.

Bears have short, fur-covered tails.

Giant Panda

Fur for Disguise

The giant panda's extraordinary fur coat is black and white. In its natural environment – deep forests and high, snowy slopes – its colouring helps to disguise it. Its striking fur may also send a clear message to other pandas to stay away. The black eye patches make its eyes look huge, giving it a frightening stare.

Not all moles have black fur – some are brown or even creamy white in colour.

Mole

Fur for Protection

Moles spend their lives underground, away from the warmth of the sun. Fur keeps these animals warm, and also protects their skin from being cut or scraped while they are tunnelling through the rocky earth.

Fur for Warmth

The Arctic polar bear can cope in colder temperatures than any other mammal, thanks its thick fur coat. The fur's white colour helps the polar bear blend in with the snowy landscape when it is hunting.

Polar Bear

The fur on the back of the front legs is long and shaggy.

FASCINATING FURRY FACTS •

Around the Arctic Ocean, the temperature on land can be as low as –60°C (–76°F), but the sea never falls below 0°C (32°F).

Underneath their white fur, polar bears have black skin.

How Does Fur Work?

Fur keeps mammals warm by providing a layer of *insulation*: a barrier that reduces the amount of heat that can escape. Fur also stops an animal's skin from coming into contact with the cold air.

DID YOU KNOW?

Wild yaks live higher up than other mammals. They live in the Himalayas at heights of up to 6,000 metres (19,800 feet).

Up Close

Fur usually contains two different types of hair. Longer hairs make up the outer fur. These are called *guard hairs*. The guard hairs cover the shorter, finer hairs of the undercoat. Pockets of warm air get trapped between the hairs of the undercoat. This is what makes fur so warm.

Long, fine hairs are found on the underside of the goat's neck.

The hair around the goat's feet is short to stop it from getting wet.

Angora Goat

The soft hairs of the angora goat are used to make a fabric called *mohair*.

A single sheep can produce more than 6.8 kg (15 lbs) of wool each year.

The tangled hairs of the fleece trap pockets of air to keep the animal warm.

Domestic Cow

Goat Undercoat

The angora goat's fleece has many fine undercoat hairs, so it is very soft. The skin of sheep and goats produces natural oil that keeps the fur waterproof. This oil makes the hairs stick together in tangles.

Thick or Thin?

Every mammal has fur that is well suited to its environment. Wild cattle usually have thick undercoats, because they spend the entire year outdoors. Domestic cattle (like the cow above) are given shelter during the cold winters. They tend to have thinner coats made up of many short guard hairs.

What Is Fur Made From?

Fur is made from thousands of hairs growing closely together. Although the hairs grow from the outer layer of skin, they are actually made from a non-living substance called *keratin*.

The size and shape of hair scales differ greatly among animals. Experts can identify an animal from a single hair.

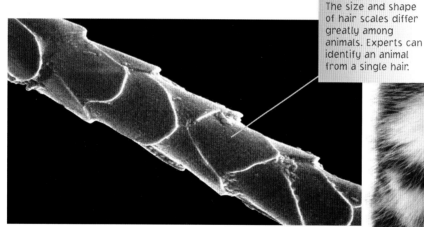

Magnified Cat Hair

Scales

The picture above shows a cat hair that has been magnified more than one hundred times. Hundreds of tiny, overlapping scales cover the surface of the hair. These scales show the direction of the hair growth. In this case, the hair has grown from left to right. Underneath the scales, the centre of the hair is hollow.

Guard hairs can be seen sticking up above the rest of the fur.

Tabby Cat

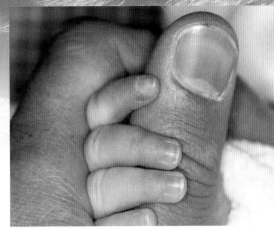

Human Fingernail

Solid Fur

Hair, nails and claws are all made from a hard material called *keratin*. Keratin is also found in most reptile scales. It is made by living things, but it is not a living material. Nails grow the same way that hair grows: material builds up under the skin until it is finally pushed outwards.

Millions of Hairs

A cat has millions of hairs covering its body. Each hair grows from a tiny hole called a *follicle*. The hair itself is not living, but each follicle is connected to living nerves, blood vessels and muscles in the cat's skin.

A cat's fur and claws are made from the same non-living material.

Can Fur Change Colour?

Like many mammals, the Arctic fox has less fur on its head and face than on the rest of its body.

Some mammals change their fur coats with the seasons. As winter approaches, their fur gets thicker and warmer. When the snow melts in spring, they shed their winter coats. In some cases, the new fur grows in a different colour.

DID YOU KNOW?

When animals shed their winter coats, the hairs drop out or are removed by scratching or licking. This is called *moulting*.

Antarctica is too cold for land mammals. The only mammals in the Antarctic are whales and seals.

FASCINATING FURRY FACT

The coat of the snowshoe hare changes colour with the season, but the tips of its ears are always black.

Snowy Coat

In winter, the coat of the Arctic fox is almost completely white. Its undercoat grows twice as thick, making the guard hairs of the outer fur stand out so the fox looks very fluffy. In summer, its coat is a grey-brown, and it lies much flatter against its body.

The stoat's nose and eyes are the only parts of its body not covered by white fur.

Stoat in Winter

Stoat Coats

Some mammals spend the winter in a long sleep, called *hibernation*. Others, such as the stoat, remain active during the winter. The stoat's thick, white winter coat is sometimes known as *ermine*. As well as keeping the animal warm, the white winter coat helps the stoat hide in the snowy landscape. In summer, the fur on the stoat's head, back and legs is brown, so it blends in with the vegetation. But the animal's belly, which usually cannot be seen, keeps its pale winter colour.

Arctic Fox

A fuller undercoat means that more warm air pockets will be trapped.

Stoat in Summer

17

Is All Fur the Same?

The quills are long and sharp enough to cause serious injury.

Not all fur is soft and fluffy. A few mammals are protected by a strange type of fur that is sharp and pointy.

Hedgehog

Quill Protection

The crested porcupine has the most extreme type of fur. Instead of hairs, it has long, sharp, hollow spines along its back and tail. These spines are called *quills*. This porcupine lives in an underground burrow. Any predator that tries to follow it down its burrow will get a face full of sharp quills.

Spiny Ball

The hedgehog is a small, insect-eating mammal. It has a coat of short, sharp spines on its neck, back and sides. Its head, legs and belly are covered with ordinary fur. When threatened by enemies, a hedgehog will curl up tightly and turn itself into a spiny ball.

The porcupine has normal fur on its head, neck and legs.

Porcupine

FASCINATING FURRY FACT

Nearly two million years ago, during the ice ages, the woolly rhinoceros had a thick fur coat to keep it warm.

White Rhinoceros

DID YOU KNOW?

A hedgehog has between 5,000 and 7,000 spines.

Each spine on a hedgehog's back lasts for about a year. Then, it drops out and is replaced by a new one.

Stripes on its quills make the porcupine harder to see.

Nose Hair

A rhinoceros, like an elephant, has tough skin with a few occasional hairs. But it also has some very special hairs growing from its nose. A rhino's horn is not like the horns of other mammals. It is made from thousands of hairs growing together into a strong, sharp point.

Does Fur Make Good Sunscreen?

Fur does not just keep an animal warm. It also protects it from the sun's harmful rays. Fur acts like a natural sunscreen, protecting an animal's skin.

FASCINATING FURRY FACTS

Mole rats live in large groups called *colonies*. Each colony has a single queen and many workers.

A mole rat colony has a central chamber connected to a network of tunnels extending up to 40 metres (130 feet) in all directions.

Desert Survival

The oryx is a type of antelope that lives among the sand dunes of the open desert. Its body is covered with fur that provides a barrier against the harmful ultra-violet (UV) rays in sunlight. The oryx's fur also protects its skin from wind-blown sand.

Underground Creatures

The mole rat is an unusual mammal: it has hardly any hairs on its body. It lives in tunnels beneath the desert surface, where there is no sunlight, so it does not need fur to protect itself from the sun's rays.

Mole Rat

Antelope horns
are made of
bone. A layer
of keratin
covers the
bone.

Oryx

Night Hopper

The jerboa is a small, furry desert mammal. It is mainly active at night, when temperatures are surprisingly cool. It does not need its fur for protection against the sun; it needs it to keep warm at night. The jerboa's feet are covered with long hairs that stop it from sinking into the soft sand.

Jerboa

Fur protects the skin against insects.

Striped colours confuse attackers.

Long hairs on the tail are used to flick away flies.

DID YOU KNOW?

The oryx has a special system of blood vessels, which keep its brain slightly cooler than the rest of its body.

Is Fur Waterproof?

Most mammals get wet from time to time. Fur keeps wet animals warm. It also helps them shed water quickly to get dry.

Some seals can stay under water for up to an hour before they have to come to the surface to take a breath.

Labrador Dog

Drip Dry

Fur usually grows with the ends of the hairs pointing back and down. This allows water to run down the hairs and drip onto the ground. Some animals, like dogs, speed up this process by shaking themselves to produce a shower of water drops.

When it is wet, a seal's fur has a slippery coating that helps it slide easily through the water.

As they dry, guard hairs form tufts that let water drain away from the rest of the fur.

Atlantic Fur Seal

Sensitive whiskers help the seal find its way in dark waters.

Thick Undercoat

Most otters live in burrows along the banks of rivers and streams. The otter has a thick undercoat of fur to keep it warm. It is so thick, and has so much trapped air, that the otter's skin remains dry while it hunts for prey under water.

Canadian Otter

FASCINATING FURRY FACTS •

Sea otters spend nearly all of their time in the water – they even sleep while floating on the water's surface.

The Brazilian giant otter can measure nearly 2 metres (6 ½ feet) long – taller than most adult men!

Fur and Fat

The southern fur seal swims in the cold waters of Antarctica. As well as a thick coat of fur on the outside, the seal has a special layer of fat beneath its skin to keep its body warm. This fat is called *blubber*.

Does Fur Make Good Camouflage?

Some fur is coloured or patterned to blend in with the background. This is called *camouflage.* Camouflage helps disguise an animal from both its predators and its prey.

The background fur along the top of the leopard's body is golden in colour.

A leopard's large, dark spots have pale centres.

White-Tail Deer Fawn

Spotted Fur

Young mammals are too slow and inexperienced to escape from predators, so they rely on camouflage to keep them safe. The coat of this deer fawn is dappled with pale spots that look like patches of sunlight.

FASCINATING FURRY FACT

Spots and stripes confuse the eye and make it difficult for attackers to see the outline of an animal.

Dazzled

Zebras' bold stripes are an example of *dazzle camouflage*. They live in large herds and their stripes make it difficult for a predator to concentrate on a single victim. The hunter becomes confused as to where one zebra ends and the next begins.

Herd of Zebras

Small spots make it difficult to see the leopard's face when it is in long grass.

The leopard has pale fur under its body and legs.

Leopard

DID YOU KNOW?

Spots are the most common fur pattern among the big cats – only tigers have stripes.

The leopard is the best climber of all the big cats. It is the only one that sleeps on tree branches.

Stripes or Spots?

There are two basic patterns on fur: stripes and spots. Some mammals have a mixture of both. The colours and patterns are found only in the fur itself – the skin underneath is usually pale and unpatterned.

Can Fur Send Messages?

Sometimes, mammals do not want to remain hidden – they want to stand out. Fur is one of the many ways that animals send messages to each other.

A stripe of white fur gives the skunk an unmistakable appearance.

Blue Burmese Kitten

Hair Raising

When mammals become angry or frightened, their fur stands on end, as shown by this Burmese kitten. The fluffed-up fur makes the cat look bigger than it really is. It sends a message that the animal is fully alert and ready for action.

Skunk

Crested porcupines rattle their quills together to send messages to other porcupines.

FASCINATING FURRY FACT

DID YOU KNOW?

A skunk can spray its foul-smelling liquid over distances of up to 3 metres (10 feet).

The spotted skunk does a handstand and walks with its back legs in the air before spraying.

Stink Alert

The black and white stripes on a skunk's fur are an unmistakable message that this animal is best left alone. When angry or frightened, a skunk squirts a jet of foul-smelling substance from under its tail.

This raised tail is an obvious warning that the skunk is about to unleash a smelly liquid.

This flash of white fur warns other deer that danger is near.

Warning Flash

Some mammals, like rabbits and deer, have a stripe of white fur beneath their tails. When frightened, these animals raise their tails and run away, revealing the flash of pale fur to serve as a warning to others.

White-Tail Deer

Does Fur need Special Care?

Fur must be kept in good condition. Mammals keep their fur clean and healthy through constant grooming.

Long fur needs lots of attention to keep it free from tangles.

DID YOU KNOW?

Rabbits spend about 16 hours a day safe in their underground burrows.

Rabbits stay the same colour all year round, unlike mountain hares, whose fur turns white in winter.

Rabbit

Regular Care

Grooming is very important. Many mammals spend hours each day grooming themselves and each other. Any tangles and plant seeds are combed out of the fur. Particular attention is paid to faces and whiskers.

Fleas and other parasites attach themselves to the skin beneath the fur.

Older chimps have dark faces, while younger chimps' faces are pale.

Chimpanzees

Bay Horse

Grooming Group

For many animals, grooming is a group activity. Here, an adult chimp examines the head of a younger chimp for fleas, while another young chimp grooms the adult's back.

Dry Bath

Sometimes, animals with short coats take a dry bath by rolling around in the dirt. This might not seem like a good way to keep clean, but it works. Rolling on the ground rubs grains of dirt into the fur to remove parasites.

FASCINATING FURRY FACTS

Chimpanzees are not monkeys; they are apes, and are most closely related to gorillas and humans.

Chimps use simple tools to get food. They use long, thin sticks to collect ants from ant-hills.

Glossary

Blubber

The thick fat found in a layer under the skin of seals and whales.

Camouflage

Colouration or patterns that help an animal blend in with its surroundings. This makes it hard for attackers to see the animal.

Domesticated

Describes plants and animals that have been changed to suit human requirements.

Endangered

In danger of extinction.

Fleece

The tangled fur coat of sheep and goats.

Follicle

A tiny hole in the skin from which a hair grows.

Guard Hairs

The longer, thicker hairs that make up the outer part of animal's coat.

Insulation

A substance that reduces the amount of heat that is lost.

Keratin

A hard material produced in the skin of animals that makes up the nails, hair and horns.

Mammal

An animal with an internal skeleton arranged around a backbone. It breathes air through lungs and feeds its young on milk. Its skin is usually protected by fur.

Moulting

The process by which mammals shed their winter undercoats.

Parasite

An animal or plant that lives and feeds on the body of another living thing.

Predator

Any animal that hunts and eats other animals.

Prey

Any animal that is hunted and eaten by others.

Quill

A long, straight spine that grows on the back of a porcupine.

Skin

The soft, stretchy substance that covers the bodies of animals. Skin is usually protected by fur, feathers, scales or slime.

Ultra-Violet (UV)

The harmful rays contained in sunlight. Too much ultra-violet energy can cause permanent damage to skin.

Undercoat

The short, fine hairs that make up the inner part of a mammal's fur coat.

Wool

The thick coat of fur that covers sheep and goats

Picture Credits

Index